First English edition published by Colour Library Books Ltd.
© 1984 Illustrations and text: Colour Library Books Ltd.,
   Guildford, Surrey, England.
This edition published by Crescent Books.
Distributed by Crown Publishers, Inc.
hgfedcba
   Richmond, Surrey, England.
Colour separations by Llovet S.A., Barcelona, Spain.
Printed and bound in Barcelona, Spain by Rieusset and Gráficas Estella.
ISBN 0 517 46277 X
CRESCENT 1984

BRUCE SPRINGSTEEN

by
Michael Stewart

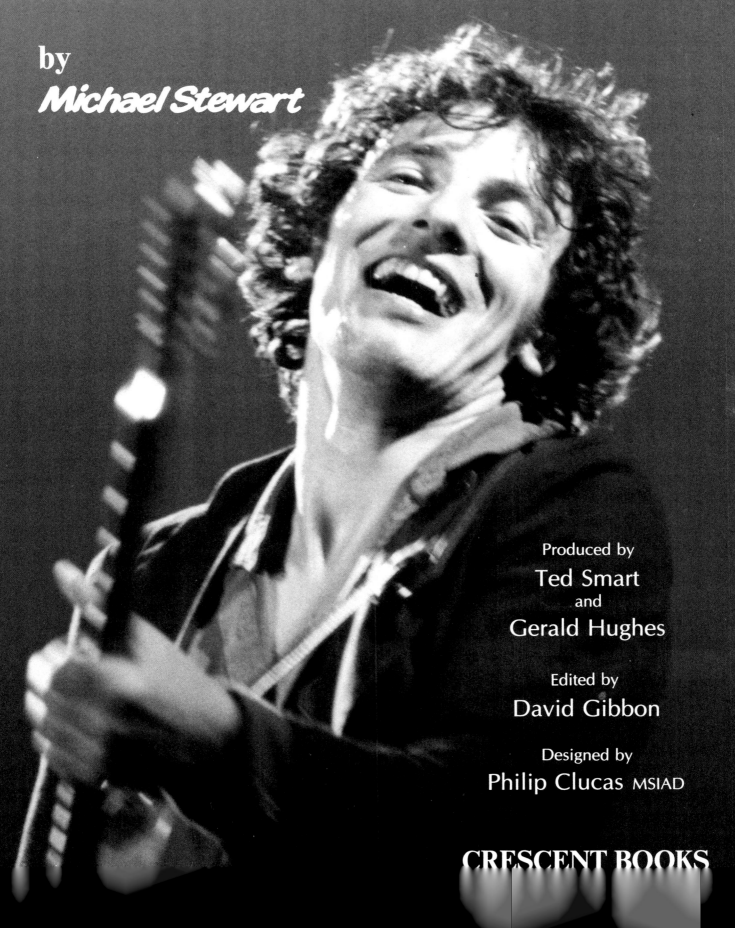

Produced by
Ted Smart
and
Gerald Hughes

Edited by
David Gibbon

Designed by
Philip Clucas MSIAD

CRESCENT BOOKS

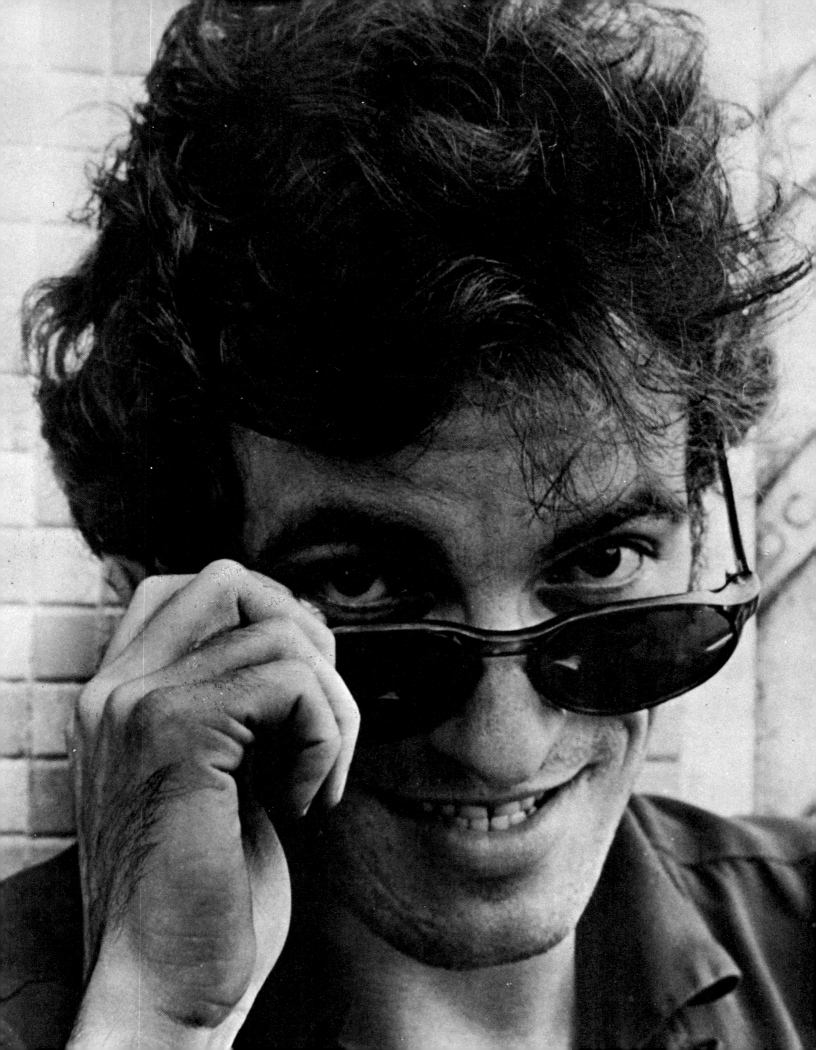

Bruce Springsteen is the most brilliant American rock and roll performer of the last decade. It's a combination of his considerable talent, his excellent band, and his obvious integrity that has made him into one of the top concert draws in the world.

Everywhere he goes he inspires a near religious adulation. His concerts are considered miracles and his records are received like manna from heaven. He compounds a sparkling, romantic vision of epic proportions from a vantage point of the back alleys of night-time New Jersey, and molds it to some of the most exhilarating rock and roll since the fifties.

Bruce Springsteen represents nearly four decades of American tradition. He has an acute love of black sixties soul which is usually meshed with the primal depths of his white rock and roll roots; add to this the muscular heritage of America — beat,

country and western, dustbowl folk music, rockabilly and blues.

It wouldn't mean much if it wasn't delivered with the most awesomely powerful live performance rock music can ever hope to achieve. Even a giant stadium is reduced to a sweaty morass of ecstacy, seduced by the man's intimacy and the warmth and strength of his sound.

In 1981 he embarked on his first full British tour. It was against a musical climate that was drastically fragmented. One

figurehead couldn't be expected to unite such a diverse spectrum. At the very least, though, he could serve as a focus for a shared belief in music's essential values.

With the minimum of fanfare, and at a time when the music press were concerned to an obsessive degree with the ludicrous conceits and narcissism of the New Romantic cult, Bruce Springsteen proved to be the largest concert draw in the whole world. Few could have predicted that a performer whose very being was obsessively stuck on rock music's most traditional elements could have won over the minds, bodies and souls of a whole nation.

Bruce Springsteen And The E Street Band had left Shea's Buffalo Theater on May 23, 1978 and completed 109 shows before over one million people – with only a month off – by the end of 1978. He was back on stage on October 3, 1980 at Ann Arbor, Michigan, before the release of his fifth album – The River – to start yet another exhausting trek around America.

Don't get to thinking that it's just a quick hour set and then off. Bruce Springsteen plays an average set lasting four hours. The mental and physical strain took its toll when he collapsed and delayed the British and European dates by three months.

Despite never having a hit single in Great Britain, nor recent promotion over the usual media of radio and television, 300,000 people applied for 105,000 seats.

Almost simultaneously, an East Coast

Jones as featured vocalist, the folk-rock of The Byrds, the power of The Who's frenetic singles. In those days the radio was full of mystery, rather than the pre-programed spoonfeeding you get nowadays. There was the orchestral paranoia of Phil Spector and Roy Orbison and the raucous energy of Gary 'US' Bonds. But it wasn't just classics. It was just as important that Bruce gobbled up the hundreds of trashy, second line performers of sixties rhythm and blues. Many of the richest vocal and instrumental effects in his later work derived from the likes of Mitch Ryder, the Young Rascals and Gary 'US' Bonds.

radio announcement concerning a concert to inaugurate the new 20,000 seater stadium in New Jersey, coupled with a few bars of 'Born To Run', the State anthem, drew an awesome half million ticket requests in only two days. Springsteen's name hadn't even been mentioned.

It was not the best time for rock and roll heroism. By the middle seventies, many Americans were languishing in a mood of spiritual exhaustion, a predictable response to the debacles of the Vietnam War and the Watergate scandals. The sense of desperation and torpor had become so commonplace that a president had proclaimed it an age of malaise. Popular music, by then a booming, multi-billion dollar industry, mirrored the feelings and exploited them, offering audiences an array of glossy palliatives. In this setting, many rock fans placed their hopes in Bruce Springsteen, an artist who seemed to resist the drift towards escapism, to reclaim rock and roll's vitality and to blaze a more daring musical path.

He was born in Freehold, New Jersey on September 23, 1949, the first child of Adele and Douglas Springsteen. He later acquired two sisters, Ginny and Pam. The surname is Dutch, not Jewish as is normally supposed. Douglas Springsteen's ancestry is mostly Irish, his wife is Italian. Bruce claims his talent for tale-spinning – so much a feature of his songs and stage shows – is derived from his maternal Grandfather Zirilli.

His father was a bus driver who wanted his son to go to college and become a lawyer. But at the age of 13 Bruce was seized with a passion for rock and roll, and the guitar. Bruce's first exposure to the music was seeing Elvis on the popular American TV variety programme The Ed Sullivan Show. Like Bruce, Elvis had a background that offered neither financial support nor hope.

"Man, when I was nine, I couldn't imagine anybody not wanting to be Elvis Presley," he later said. He got so transfixed by the image

of Elvis Presley that he got his mother to buy him a guitar. But he was too small in the hands, lessons were worse than torture and it never sounded the way Elvis did it. The guitar remained on the shelf for nearly five years.

"I was dead until I was thirteen," says Bruce. It was then that lightning struck and he discovered the magic that he could weave with a guitar. Since that day, Bruce has said: "Rock and Roll has been everything to me. The first day I can remember looking into a mirror and being able to stand what I saw was the day I had a guitar in my hand."

The radio became his encyclopedia of music. He bought few records except those that he wanted to learn to play.

He loved the classic artists: Elvis Presley, Chuck Berry, The Beatles, The Rolling Stones, Eric Burdon And The Animals, Manfred Mann's early records with Paul

After playing in a few bands in his local area, he heard about the music scene at nearby Asbury Park – a small-time beach town. It was dismal by most standards. The Downtown area is nearly empty, devastated by municipal default in the thirties, urban renewal in the fifties and a race riot in the seventies. Turn east, cross the railroad tracks and life picks up – but not by much. On the boardwalk there's Madam Marie's – mentioned on *4th Of July, Asbury Park (Sandy)* and a few other songs.

The real attraction of Asbury Park had nothing to do with the beach. The draw for musicians was a club called The Upstage, which had two sessions on weekends, one from eight to midnight and another from one to five in the morning. Bruce remembered the place in his liner notes for the first Southside Johnny And The Asbury Jukes album, *I Don't Want To Go Home.*

"There were a lotta musicians there 'cause the bands that came down from North Jersey and New York to play in the Top 40 clubs along the shore would usually end up there after their regular gig, along with a lotta different guys from the local areas. Everybody went there 'cause it was open later than the regular clubs and because between one and five in the morning you could play pretty much whatever you wanted, and if you were good enough, you could choose the guys you wanted to play with.

"The Upstage was run by this beat type guy named Tom Potter who plastered the walls with black light and pin-ups and showed '50s smokers to the kids in between the bands . . . It was a great place. He'd slip you five or ten bucks to sit in, and you could work it so you'd never have to go home, 'cause by the time you got out of there it was dawn and you could flop on the beach all day, or could run home before it got too light, nail the blankets over the windows of your room, and just sleep straight through all the night.

"There were these guys . . . Mad Dog Lopez, Big Danny, Fast Eddie Larachi, his brother Little John, Margaret & The Distractions (house band), Black Tiny, White Tiny, Miami Steve, and assorted E Streeters, plus the heaviest drummer of them all, in terms of both poundage and sheer sonic impact, Biiiiig Baaaaad Bobby Williams, badass king of hearts, so tough he'd go to the limit for you every time, all night.

"You will never see most of these names again on another record besides this one, but nonetheless, they're names that should be spoken in reverence at least once, not 'cause they were great musicians (truth is, some of them couldn't play nothin' at all), but because they were each in their own way a living spirit of what, to me, rock and roll is all about. It was music as survival, and they lived it down in their souls, night after night. These guys were their own heroes, and they never forgot."

The Jersey shore's isolation was an advantage to Bruce Springsteen's development. He was able to develop a style

Southside Johnny And The Asbury Jukes were laid. In the process he found pianist and guitarist David Sancious, bassist Garry Tallent, Miami Steve Van Zandt, his long-time guitar foil, Vini 'Mad Dog' Lopez on drums and organist Danny Federici.

The band quickly broke up because of its size but it was soon playing dates as a five piece. But that didn't work, so Bruce had to try it as a solo artist. His eccentric solo act was full of verbose songs that mocked his painful Catholic past.

A pair of songwriters, Mike Appel and Jim Cretecos, saw Bruce and were impressed. Bruce was impressed with them – they'd written a hit for top teeny-bop group The Partridge Family. Bruce signed a long-term management deal with Appel. Appel managed to fix Bruce with an audition with John Hammond.

Hammond was famous for finding Bob Dylan. But his history of talent scouting went way beyond that. He had 'discovered' Bessie Smith, he was responsible for signing Billie Holliday to Columbia in 1938, he had recorded Aretha Franklin in the fifties. His place in music history was secure.

He got Bruce to play for him. "I couldn't

that was free from the pressure of trends and false criteria about what was hip. Springsteen was able to concentrate on and explore music that elsewhere was forgotten.

Bruce quickly absorbed styles and influences and became more than just a human jukebox but a human synthesiser, with an enormous repertoire of songs, fragments of half remembered hits and a facility to learn quickly from the radio. He built his songs on this half memory, which gave all his original songs a familiar feel on first hearing. Bruce was able to shape his rock dreams into a strong and powerful vision that was genuinely original.

Bruce was soon co-opted into a band called Steel Mill. They played in California to rave reviews. It was Bruce's first time out of New Jersey. In 1970 Bruce let the band fold and formed Dr. Zoom and the Sonic Boom in 1971. He wanted to form a band with ten pieces, including horns and girl singers. While rehearsing for this band he put together a group featuring all the Asbury Park people who weren't in other bands – this was Dr. Zoom and the Sonic Boom. They played three dates, including one supporting the Allman Brothers Band. The group changed nightly. They even set up a Monopoly table in the middle of the stage.

"That was to give the people who didn't play anything a chance to be in the band," says Bruce later. "You know, so they could say, 'Yeah, I'm in Dr. Zoom, I play Monopoly.'"

But it was the ten piece band – known as The Bruce Springsteen Band – that held more importance for Bruce. It was here that the foundations of both his present band and

believe it," says Hammond. "I reacted with a force I've felt maybe three times in my life. I knew at once that he would last a generation."

Hammond was mightily impressed with intense and enigmatic tunes like *Arabian Nights, Growin' Up, If I Was The Priest* and *Southern Son;* he signed up Bruce immediately.

But there were troubles straight out. The scope of Bruce Springsteen's songwriting abilities led to a misconception of his talent. John Hammond pictured him as a solo performer (as did Appel), although he had a few ideas about expanding Springsteen's natural charisma beyond the traditional singer-songwriter image. This confusion resulted in Columbia dreaming up a promotion based on the lines of Bruce being the new Dylan.

Cretecos and Appel simply didn't realize the rock and roll inherent in Springsteen's songs, and the singer's own ignorance of the studio resulted in the restrained sound of his first album *Greetings From Asbury Park, NJ,* released in 1973.

Springsteen had played *It's Hard To Be A Saint In The City* for John Hammond with a clear idea of the tune as a rock number. Yet the version on *Greetings From Asbury Park, NJ* (a last minute replacement for the anti-

war *American Tune,* which made it onto some promotional copies) fades on the final chorus, precisely where in concert the song develops into a fierce guitar duel between Bruce Springsteen and Miami Steve Van Zandt.

Many of the conflicts and problems of image surrounding his music was abetted by Springsteen himself. At any given moment Danny Federici would change from organ to accordion and Garry Tallent from bass to tuba. Springsteen didn't discard all his folkie tendencies until 1974 and his eclecticism often led to a disjointed show. But it was this drive, this push towards a personal musical structure that was his greatest strength.

He took his discoveries and edited them down, channelling and focusing his forays into rock's vast tapestry into a dynamic, increasingly simple form. Tunes rolled off his pen and arrangements changed often. More and more, he remolded his image from wordy performer to Boss, the E Street Band leader, a role reflected in ever-increasing soul influences.

He wrote songs that depended for impact on a flow of obscure but enticing words. But more and more his writing reflected old soul influences and his storytelling power revealed itself in tales of kids living out

desperate lives. His ambition led him to take on the dreams and hopes of the biggest city of them all on 1973s *The Wild, The Innocent And The E Street Shuffle.*

The city, its characters and a fascination with sound dominated *The Wild, The Innocent And The E Street Shuffle.* Bruce Springsteen's innate feel for street scenes and human relationships reached a peak. The songs were intimately linked conceptually. Side two of the album was practically a suite, beginning and ending with scenes of urban poverty and romance *(Incident On 57th Street, New York City Serenade);* the rock anthem *Rosalita,* a hilarious statement of purpose, is sandwiched between them.

The record received all the acclaim the rock press could deliver but it was a commercial flop. One of the critics, Jon Landau, was to have a bearing on Bruce Springsteen's future. He wrote a review that was complimentary about the music but

criticized the 'fuzzy' production. He later saw Bruce and Appel and explained his reservations. The same day he saw Bruce's show and wrote a legendary review for the Loose Ends column in *Rolling Stone* magazine about his experience.

"It's four in the morning and raining," he began. "I'm 27 today, feeling old, listening to my records and remembering that things were different a decade ago . . ."

"But tonight there is someone I can write of the way I used to write, without reservations of any kind. Last Thursday at Harvard Square Theater, I saw my rock and roll past flash past my eyes. And I saw something else. I saw rock and roll's future and its name is Bruce Springsteen. And on a night when I needed to feel young he made me feel like I was hearing music for the first time."

Everywhere Bruce Springsteen And The E Street Band appeared, audiences responded

with wild enthusiasm. A devoted cult following in several cities began to insist that, as judged by his live performances, Bruce was indeed the new voice the nation had been waiting for.

Springsteen in concert is an undeniably impressive figure. He paces back and forth across the stage, striking dramatic chords on his guitar and urging the E Street Band on. By now it had settled on a line up: Garry Tallent on bass; Danny Federici on organ; Roy Bittan on piano; Max Weinberg on drums and Clarence Clemons on saxophone. Miami Steve Van Zandt was later to join the group on guitar.

The music moves through an ascending series of climaxes in which the central themes and textures of rock are displayed in grand conjunction. Although the songs are tightly arranged and executed, they flow gracefully, quenching the audience's thirst for a stiff, rugged sound. Bruce's vocals range freely across the broad spectrum from soft,

plaintive moans to clipped, assertive chants to intense, exalting cries. His horn section, patterned on the great Stax and Junior Walker records of yesteryear, embroider the lyric with riffs and solos that hone the music's sharp edge. Playing exceptionally long sets, Springsteen reawakened archetypal American fantasies – freedom experienced through flight; love powerful enough to conquer desperate loneliness; brotherhood forged by danger in the streets; good outlaws chased by bad cops; the hero as an isolated individual, running, running, always running.

Landau's review changed the lives of both writer and artist. Columbia, Bruce's record label, immediately grasped the publicity value of the review and reprinted it widely throughout the press. Several months later Landau was signed to co-produce the next Springsteen album, a work of lofty intentions that Bruce had been struggling to finish.

By the time *Born To Run*, his third album, was released in Autumn 1975, music industry excitement about the Springsteen phenomenon had built to such a high pitch that both American news magazines, the influential *Time* and *Newsweek*, ran cover stories on the making of the new star. The album soon achieved both commercial success and critical acclaim. After many fits and starts, the young rocker had finally arrived.

Born To Run was a concept album in every important sense – its Phil Spector-influenced production gave it continuity of sound, and the progression from the opening *Thunder Road* to the final *Jungleland* was really one long story. But in achieving this ferocious attack of purpose, Springsteen sacrificed nothing and made no concessions to non-rock: *Born To Run,* the record's hit single, is the crust of classic rock and roll, and numbers like *Backstreets, She's The One,* and *Tenth Avenue Freeze-Out* dig even deeper. *Born To Run* was an assertion that he could do it all, that he wasn't just a rocker but a truly great one – one with a clarity of purpose and a mammoth ambition.

The tour that followed received Bruce like the new messiah. His impressively poetic grasp of the preoccupations of an East Coast small-town teenager: oppressive work by day, hard-to-find good times by night, the emptiness of the movie-engendered myths the kids tried to live up to, the rackets, the gangs, and the half-grasped, half-doubted possibility of escape with your best girl in the passenger, was hard to resist, even by non-converts and those whose scepticism was raised by the relentless hype and the passion by which disciples spoke in reverence about their new rock and roll hero.

Springsteen's career was halted by litigation with his manager Mike Appel which prevented him from recording. But he used the time to help inaugurate the recording career of Southside Johnny And The Asbury Jukes. Also, one of his compositions, *Blinded By The Light*, reached number one in the American singles charts by Manfred Mann's Earth Band. But it cost Bruce Springsteen nearly three years of time to sort out his legal problems.

Bruce Springsteen returned in the Spring of 1978 with *Darkness On The Edge Of Town* and a new manager in Jon Landau. The album, his fourth, has an aura of gloom and futility surrounding it, and may well reflect the legal hassles and their resultant frustrations.

Darkness On The Edge Of Town rejected the production embellishments of *Born To Run* for a hard-nosed sound driven by Springsteen's furious guitar and aching vocals. On it, the E Street Band could finally be heard as one of the best supporting combos in rock music. More importantly, Bruce Springsteen's music and lyrics told stories that meant he'd begun to mature. The bite of *Darkness On The Edge Of Town* makes *Born To Run* look positively mushy as Bruce Springsteen asserts himself as a guitarist in the fiery spirit of Led Zeppelin's Jimmy Page or Jimi Hendrix. In the lyrics, he gives evidence of a perspective that is newly mature and more deeply compassionate than his earlier fantasies of the sweet life. It's an album of revenge, but revenge filled with innocence, hope and compassion. Springsteen asserts both the pain of lost innocence and the ache of a hope against hope.

In September 1979 he played a concert for MUSE – Musicians For Safe Energy – an anti-nuclear group, far stronger after the near disaster of Three Mile Island. It was the only gig he played between the Darkness On The Edge Of Town Tour and the opening in 1980 of his The River Tour.

The River was his fifth album, a double set which coursed through a dozen styles: the rockabilly nuances of *Cadillac Ranch,* the Stones-like raunch of *Crush On You,* the Searchers beat of *The Ties That Bind,* the folk rock of *The River,* the country and western voice of *Wreck On The Highway,* and the ballads that seemingly derived from Bob Dylan or Van Morrison but are now recognizably Springsteen's: *Stolen Car, Point Blank, The Price You Pay* and *Independence Day.*

On the surface the songs and themes weren't that different from those Springsteen had told before. It was only when you sliced beneath the surface of the songs themselves that the sadness in a rocker like *Cadillac Ranch* comes out. The wild rebels don't seem so innocent, young and bold any more, but naive, crazy and terribly vulnerable. The people in the songs are older, tied to jobs or looking for work, and it's the jobs – or joblessness – that dominate. No one is transcending anything; everybody's too busy just trying to get on with their lives. *The River* is about inescapable realities, including the reality of always trying to escape and always falling back.

The tour that followed took Bruce
Springsteen And The E Street Band across
America more than once, and eventually
took them to Europe, Japan, Australia and
back home to New Jersey. Almost
everywhere the audience greeted him with a
fierce devotion; crowds sang his songs for
him and picked up on his every movement.
The stars in each port of call came away
convinced. The show grew from three
hours to four, and more if the occasion was
deemed special.

He followed up the rich color of *The River*
with the solo set *Nebraska*. It was an album
created in 1982 with just Bruce, a guitar and
a harmonica, recorded on a Portastudio (a
portable tape recorder) and nothing else. The
images of America that he conjured up were
similar to Woody Guthrie's insights into the
dustbowl depression of the thirties. It was a
monochromatic film record of the sights and
sounds of the road. It was an impressive
work that won much critical acclaim but had
only minor commercial success.

It wasn't until the seventh album – *Born In
The USA* – released in 1984 – that Bruce
Springsteen and the E Street Band reaped
their astonishing popularity when his album
hit number one in both Britain and America
and his single *Dancing In The Dark* reached
number two in the U.S. singles chart.

If there's a central theme to the career of Bruce Springsteen that shows up his dedication to rock and roll, then it is best summed up by this story that he told on stage during his 1978 tour.

"When I was growing up, there were two things that were unpopular in my house. One was me and the other was my guitar. We had this grate, like the heat was supposed to come through, except it wasn't hooked up to any of the heating ducts; it was just open straight down to the kitchen, and there was a gas stove right underneath it. When I used to start playing, my pop used to turn on the gas jets and try to smoke me out of the room. And I had to go hide out on the roof or something.

"He always used to call the guitar, never Fender guitar or Gibson guitar, it was always the God-damned guitar. Everytime he'd knock on my door, that was all I would hear: 'Turn down that God-damned guitar.' He must have thought everything in my room was the same brand: God-damned guitar, God-damned stereo, God-damned radio.

"Anyway, one day my mom and pop, they come up to me and say, 'Bruce, it's time to get serious with your life. This guitar thing ... it's OK as a hobby but you need something to fall back on.' My father, he said, 'You should be a lawyer, they run the world.'

"My mother says I should be an author. But me I wanted to play guitar.

"Since this was an important thing they sent me to the priest but told me not to say anything about the God-damned guitar. So I went to the rectory and talked to Father Ray. He said it was too big for him and I should see God. Tell him about the lawyer and the author but say nothing about that guitar.

"Now I was worried. Where was I going to find God, right? So I go to find Clarence – he knows everybody. Clarence says 'no sweat,' and took me to God's place.

"So we drive out of town, along this old dark road. We drive a long ways, and I say to Clarence, 'Man, you sure you know where you're going?' Clarence says 'Sure, I just took a guy out here the other day.' So we finally come to this little house, way out in the woods, nothing around, but the lights are on inside. There's music blasting out and a little hole in the door.

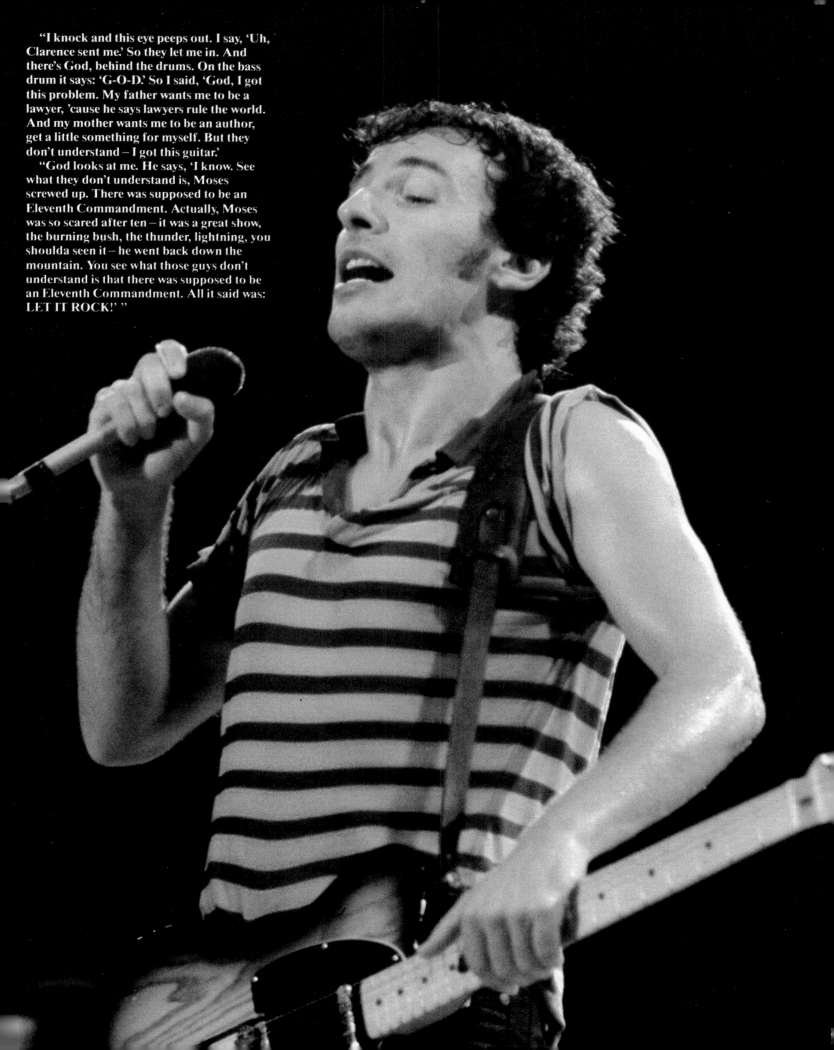

"I knock and this eye peeps out. I say, 'Uh, Clarence sent me.' So they let me in. And there's God, behind the drums. On the bass drum it says: 'G-O-D.' So I said, 'God, I got this problem. My father wants me to be a lawyer, 'cause he says lawyers rule the world. And my mother wants me to be an author, get a little something for myself. But they don't understand – I got this guitar.'

"God looks at me. He says, 'I know. See what they don't understand is, Moses screwed up. There was supposed to be an Eleventh Commandment. Actually, Moses was so scared after ten – it was a great show, the burning bush, the thunder, lightning, you shoulda seen it – he went back down the mountain. You see what those guys don't understand is that there was supposed to be an Eleventh Commandment. All it said was: LET IT ROCK!' "

DISCOGRAPHY

Albums

GREETINGS FROM ASBURY PARK, N.J.
(CBS 65480) – 1973

Blinded By The Light; Growin' Up; Mary, Queen Of Arkansas; Does This Bus Stop at 32nd Street?; Lost In The Flood; The Angel; For You; Spirit In The Night; It's Hard To Be A Saint In The City.

THE WILD, THE INNOCENT AND THE E STREET SHUFFLE
(CBS 65780) – 1973

The E Street Shuffle; 4th Of July, Asbury Park (Sandy); Kitty's Back; Wild Billy's Circus Story; Incident On 57th Street; Rosalita (Come Out Tonight); New York City Serenade.

BORN TO RUN
(CBS 69170) – 1975

Thunder Road; Tenth Avenue Freeze-Out; Night; Backstreets; Born To Run; She's The One; Meeting Across The River; Jungleland.

DARKNESS ON THE EDGE OF TOWN
(CBS 86061) – 1978

Badlands; Adam Raised A Cain; Something In The Night; Candy's Room; Racing In The Street; The Promised Land; Factory; Streets Of Fire; Prove It All Night; Darkness On The Edge Of Town.

THE RIVER
(CBS 88510) – 1980

The Ties That Bind; Sherry Darling; Jackson Cage; Two Hearts; Independence Day; Hungry Heart; Out In The Street; Crush On You; You Can Look (But You Better Not Touch); I Wanna Marry You; The River; Point Blank; Cadillac Ranch; I'm A Rocker; Fade Away; Stolen Car; Ramrod; The Price You Pay; Drive All Night; Wreck On The Highway.

NEBRASKA
(CBS 25100) – 1982

Nebraska; Atlantic City; Mansion On The Hill; Johnny 99; Highway Patrolman; State Trooper; Used Cars; Open All Night; My Father's House; Reason To Believe.

BORN IN THE USA
(CBS 86304) – 1984

Born In The USA; Cover Me; Darlington County; Working On The Highway; Downbound Train; I'm On Fire; No Surrender; Bobby Jean; I'm Goin' Down; Glory Days; Dancing In The Dark; My Hometown.

Singles

Blinded By The Light
(Columbia A545) – 1973 (US)

Blinded By The Light/The Angel
(Columbia A5805) – 1973 (US)

Spirit In The Night/For You
(Columbia A5864) – 1973 (US)

Circus Song
(Columbia A552) – 1973 (US)

Rosalita
(Columbia A566) – 1974 (US)

Rosalita/Growin' Up/Spirit In The Night
(Columbia 1088) – 1974 (US)
(Promotional only)

Born To Run/Meeting Across The River
(Columbia 10209) – 1975 (US)
(reached number 23 in US charts)

Born To Run/Meeting Across The River
(CBS 3661) – 1975 (UK)

Tenth Avenue Freeze-Out/She's The One
(Columbia 10274) – 1975 (US)

Tenth Avenue Freeze-Out/She's The One
(CBS 3940) – 1976 (UK)

Born To Run/Spirit In The Night
(Columbia 33323) – 1976 (US)
(Hall Of Fame Series)

Born To Run/Meeting Across The River
(CBS 7077) – 1976 (UK)
(Golden Decade Series)

Prove It All Night/Factory
(Columbia 10763) – 1978 (US)
(reached number 33 in US charts)

Prove It All Night/Factory
(CBS 6424) – 1978 (UK)

Badlands/Streets Of Fire
(Columbia 10801) – 1978 (US)

Badlands/Something In The Night
(CBS 6532) – 1978 (UK)

Promised Land/Streets Of Fire
(CBS 6720) – 1978 (UK)

Hungry Heart/Held Up Without A Gun
(Columbia 11391) – 1980 (US)
(reached number 5 in US charts)

Hungry Heart/Held Up Without A Gun
(CBS 9309) – 1980 (UK)
(reached number 44 in UK charts)

Fade Away/Be True
(Columbia 11431) – 1981 (US)
(reached number 20 in US charts)

Sherry Darling/Be True
(CBS 9568) – 1981 (UK)

The River/Independence Day
(CBS 1179) – 1981 (UK)
(reached number 35 in UK charts)

Dancing In The Dark/Pink Cadillac
(Columbia   ) – 1984 (US)
(reached number 2 in US charts)

Dancing In The Dark/Pink Cadillac
(CBS A4436) – 1984 (UK)
(reached number 28 in UK charts)

Three of these records (A545, A552 and A566) were released as part of the Playback Series. This was a club formed by Columbia to try to raise interest in artists whose releases had passed almost unnoticed. Members paid a subscription fee and were sent the EPs as they were pressed. The records contained songs by more than one artist so if you bought 'Rosalita', for example, then expect to find Johnny Winter and The Hollies on the flip side.

The most interesting item is the Playback version of 'Circus Song' which was recorded live at the CBS Convention in the Ahmanson Theater, Los Angeles in 1973.

Columbia's Hall Of Fame and CBS's Golden Decade Series were re-issues of 'classic' 45s and contained singles by Santana, Fleetwood Mac, Simon and Garfunkel and Bruce Springsteen.

The Songs

This is a listing of the songs written by Bruce Springsteen. Some were written for Steel Mill or the Bruce Springsteen Band, but most have been conceived since he signed with Columbia/CBS Records.

Action In The Streets A frequent, soul-styled, stage favourite from the 1976 tours. Unreleased but titled by fans.

Adam Raised A Cain Released on Darkness On The Edge Of Town.

American Tune Unreleased; but included on the early acetates of Greetings From Asbury Park, NJ, but replaced by It's Hard To Be A Saint In The City.

Angel Released on Greetings from Asbury Park, NJ and the B-side of Blinded By The Light single.

Arabian Nights Recorded for May 1973 John Hammond demo tape, unreleased.

Atlantic City Released on Nebraska.

Backstreets Released on Born To Run.

Badlands Released on Darkness On The Edge Of Town, and as a single with Streets Of Fire in US and Something In The Night in UK.

Because The Night Written for Darkness On The Edge Of Town; unissued. Became a hit in 1978 (number 5 in UK, number 13 in US) for Patti Smith Group which was produced by Jimmy Iovine after being smuggled out of Springsteen session into Smith session next door.

Be True Recorded for The River; issued as B-side of Fade Away single.

Blinded By The Light Released on Greetings From Asbury Park, NJ, and as a first Columbia single with Angel as a B-side. A number one hit for Manfred Mann's Earth Band in US and a number 6 hit in UK in 1976. Also recorded by Hollies' singer Allan Clarke.

Bobby Jean Released on Born In The USA.

Born In The USA Title track of Springsteen's seventh album.

Born To Run Released as title track of third album; made number 23 in US. Also recorded by Allan Clarke of The Hollies.

Cadillac Ranch Released on The River.

Candy's Room Released on Darkness On The Edge Of Town.

Cover Me Released on Born In The USA.

Cowboys Of The Sun Written for Bruce Springsteen Band; recorded for Hammond demos; unissued.

Crush On You Released on The River.

Dancing In The Dark Released on Born In The USA; single went to number two in US and number 28 in UK.

Darlington County Released on Born In The USA.

Darkness On The Edge Of Town Released as fourth album title track.

Dedication Recorded by Gary 'US' Bonds as title track of Springsteen/Van Zandt produced LP in 1981.

Does This Bus Stop At 82nd Street? Released on Greetings From Asbury Park, NJ and included on Hammond demo.

Don't Look Back Recorded for Darkness On The Edge Of Town but unissued.

Downbound Train Released on Born In The USA.

Drive All Night Conceived during the Darkness sessions but later inserted into live versions of Backstreets. Released on The River.

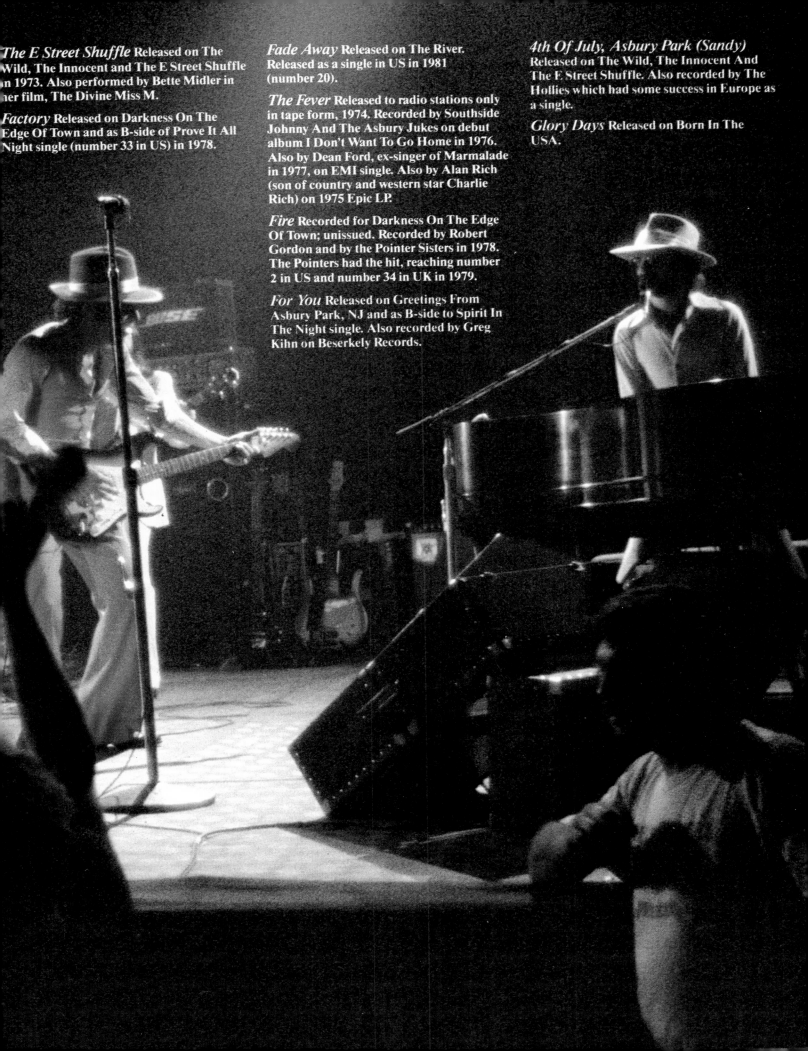

The E Street Shuffle Released on The Wild, The Innocent and The E Street Shuffle in 1973. Also performed by Bette Midler in her film, The Divine Miss M.

Factory Released on Darkness On The Edge Of Town and as B-side of Prove It All Night single (number 33 in US) in 1978.

Fade Away Released on The River. Released as a single in US in 1981 (number 20).

The Fever Released to radio stations only in tape form, 1974. Recorded by Southside Johnny And The Asbury Jukes on debut album I Don't Want To Go Home in 1976. Also by Dean Ford, ex-singer of Marmalade in 1977, on EMI single. Also by Alan Rich (son of country and western star Charlie Rich) on 1975 Epic LP.

Fire Recorded for Darkness On The Edge Of Town; unissued. Recorded by Robert Gordon and by the Pointer Sisters in 1978. The Pointers had the hit, reaching number 2 in US and number 34 in UK in 1979.

For You Released on Greetings From Asbury Park, NJ and as B-side to Spirit In The Night single. Also recorded by Greg Kihn on Beserkely Records.

4th Of July, Asbury Park (Sandy) Released on The Wild, The Innocent And The E Street Shuffle. Also recorded by The Hollies which had some success in Europe as a single.

Glory Days Released on Born In The USA.

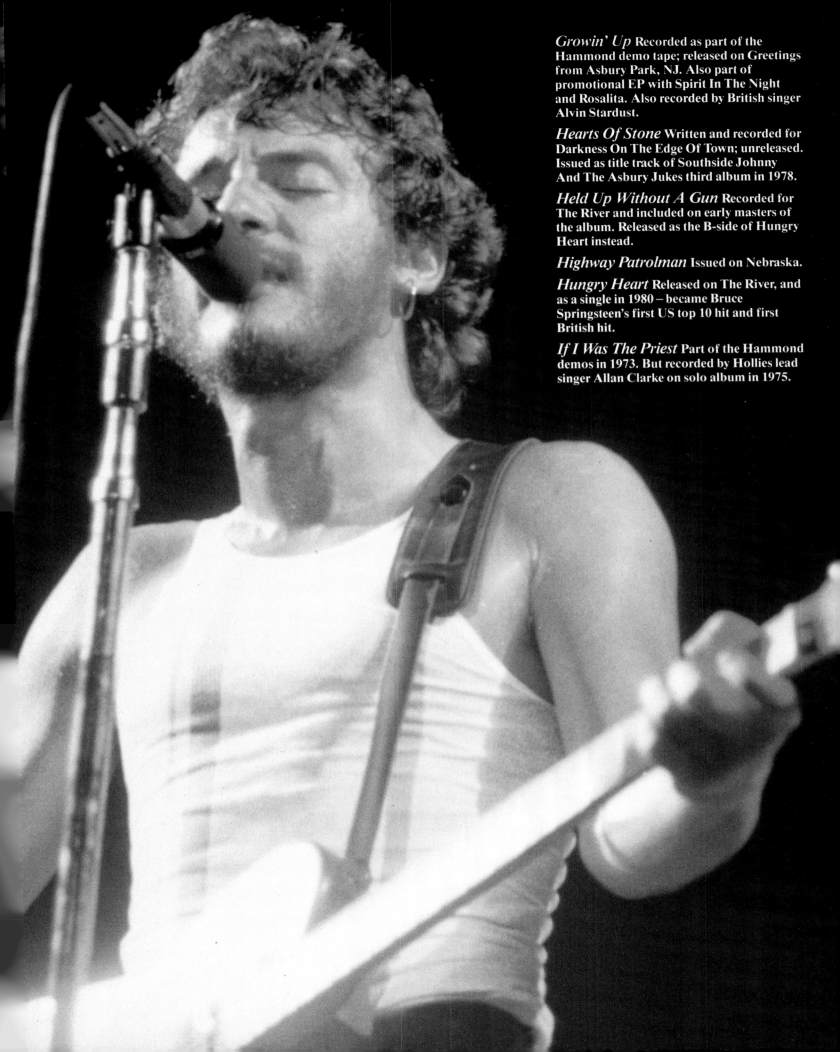

Growin' Up Recorded as part of the Hammond demo tape; released on Greetings from Asbury Park, NJ. Also part of promotional EP with Spirit In The Night and Rosalita. Also recorded by British singer Alvin Stardust.

Hearts Of Stone Written and recorded for Darkness On The Edge Of Town; unreleased. Issued as title track of Southside Johnny And The Asbury Jukes third album in 1978.

Held Up Without A Gun Recorded for The River and included on early masters of the album. Released as the B-side of Hungry Heart instead.

Highway Patrolman Issued on Nebraska.

Hungry Heart Released on The River, and as a single in 1980 – became Bruce Springsteen's first US top 10 hit and first British hit.

If I Was The Priest Part of the Hammond demos in 1973. But recorded by Hollies lead singer Allan Clarke on solo album in 1975.

I'm A Rocker Released on The River.

I'm Goin' Down Released on Born In The USA.

I'm On Fire Released on Born In The USA.

Incident on 57th Street Released on The Wild, The Innocent And The E Street Shuffle.

Independence Day Written in 1977 and recorded for Darkness On The Edge Of Town LP but never issued. It appears on The River in its original form – it wasn't re-recorded.

It's Hard To Be A Saint In The City Released on Greetings From Asbury Park, NJ.

I Wanna Be With You Recorded for both Darkness On The Edge Of Town and The River, but never released.

I Wanna Marry You Released on The River.

Jackson Cage Released on The River.

Janey Needs A Shooter Written around 1974/5. In 1979 Warren Zevon and Springsteen co-wrote another version (retaining only the chorus) and it appears on Zevon's third LP Bad Luck Streak In Dancing School.

Jazz Musician From the Hammond demos; unreleased.

Johnny 99 Released on Nebraska.

Jungleland Released on Born To Run.

Kitty's Back Released on The Wild, The Innocent And The E Street Shuffle.

Little Girl So Fine Written with Miami Steve Van Zandt for Southside Johnny And The Asbury Jukes' second album This Time It's For Real in 1977.

Lost In The Flood Released on Greetings From Asbury Park, NJ.

Love On The Wrong Side Of Town Co-written with Miami Steve Van Zandt for Southside Johnny And The Asbury Jukes' second LP This Time It's for Real in 1977.

Mansion On The Hill Released on Nebraska.

Mary, Queen Of Arkansas Recorded on Hammond demo tape; released on Greetings From Asbury Park, NJ.

Meeting Across The River Released on Born To Run as B-side to the title single.

My Hometown Released on Born In The USA.

My Father's House Released on Nebraska.

Nebraska Title track of Bruce Springsteen's sixth LP.

No Surrender Released on Born In The USA.

New York City Serenade Released on The Wild, The Innocent And The E Street Shuffle.

New York Song A regular stage song around 1974.

Night Released on Born To Run.

Open All Night Released on Nebraska.

Out In The Street Released on The River.

Paradise By The Sea Instrumental that opened the second half of the 1978 tour show. Issued to radio stations in tape form in 1978 from a live version recorded at Berkeley Community Theater.

Pink Cadillac Released as B-side to Dancing In The Dark single in 1984.

Point Blank Written during summer tour, 1978; released on The River.

The Price You Pay Released on The River.

The Promised Land Released on Darkness On The Edge Of Town.

Protection Written for Donna Summer on her 1982 album.

Prove It All Night Released on Darkness On The Edge Of Town, and as a single in 1978 reaching number 33 in US charts. Also, included on the Paradise By The Sea live radio station only tape.

Racing In The Street Recorded in many versions for Darkness On The Edge Of Town, on which it's finally released.

Ramrod Recorded for Darkness On The Edge Of Town; re-recorded and released on The River.

Reason To Believe Released on Nebraska.

Rendezvous Written in 1976 and recorded for Darkness On The Edge Of Town; unissued. Recorded by Greg Kihn on his third album Next Of Kihn in 1978.

Restless Nights Recorded for The River; unissued.

The River Title song of Bruce Springsteen's fifth album. Featured, in a live version, on the No Nukes movie and album.

Rosalita (Come Out Tonight) Released on The Wild, The Innocent And The E Street Shuffle. Issued as promo EP with Spirit In The Night and Growin' Up, and as a live promo disc.

Sherry Darling Written and recorded for Darkness On The Edge Of Town; re-recorded and released on The River, and as a single in 1981.

She's The One Released on Born To Run, and as a B-side to Tenth Avenue Freeze-Out single.

Something In The Night Released on Darkness On The Edge Of Town.

Southern Son From Hammond demo; unissued.

Spirit In The Night From Greetings From Asbury Park, NJ. Issued as a single with For You in 1973 and on promo EP with Rosalita and Growin' Up same year. Later recorded by Manfred Mann's Earth Band, who released it as a follow-up single to Blinded By The Light in 1977 and made the top 50.

State Trooper Released on Nebraska.

Stolen Car Released on The River.

Street Queen From Hammond demo.

Streets Of Fire Released on Darkness On The Edge Of Town and as B-side to Badlands.

Talk To Me Written and recorded for Darkness On The Edge Of Town; issued on Southside Johnny and The Asbury Jukes' third LP Hearts Of Stone in 1978.

Tenth Avenue Freeze-Out Issued on Born To Run, and as a single with She's The One in 1975.

This Little Girl Recorded by Gary 'US' Bonds on Dedication LP; issued as single in 1981. Reached number 43 in UK and number 11 in US.

The Ties That Bind Written and often performed on 1978 tour. Released on The River.

Thundercrack Often performed stage song from 1974.

Thunder Road Released on Born To Run and featured in No Nukes film.

Trapped Again Written with Miami Steve Van Zandt and Southside Johnny Lyon for the Asbury Jukes' third album, Hearts Of Stone. Issued as a single in 1978.

Two Hearts Two songs with the same title are known. One's on the Hammond demo. The other appears on The River.

Used Cars Released on Nebraska.

When You Dance Written for The Bruce Springsteen Band, used on Southside Johnny And The Asbury Jukes' second LP This Time It's For Real.

Wild Billy's Circus Story Released on The Wild, The Innocent And The E Street Shuffle, and on CBS promo EP, a live version from 1974 company convention.

Working On The Highway Released on Born In The USA.

Wreck On The Highway Released on The River.

You Can Look (But You Better Not Touch) Recorded in two versions, one as a rockabilly trio, other with full band for The River. Full band version issued.

You Mean So Much To Me Baby Written in 1974, not recorded until 1976, on Southside Johnny And The Asbury Jukes' debut LP I Don't Wanna Go Home, as a duet between Southside Johnny and Ronnie Spector.

Your Love Released on Gary 'US' Bonds' LP Dedication in 1981.

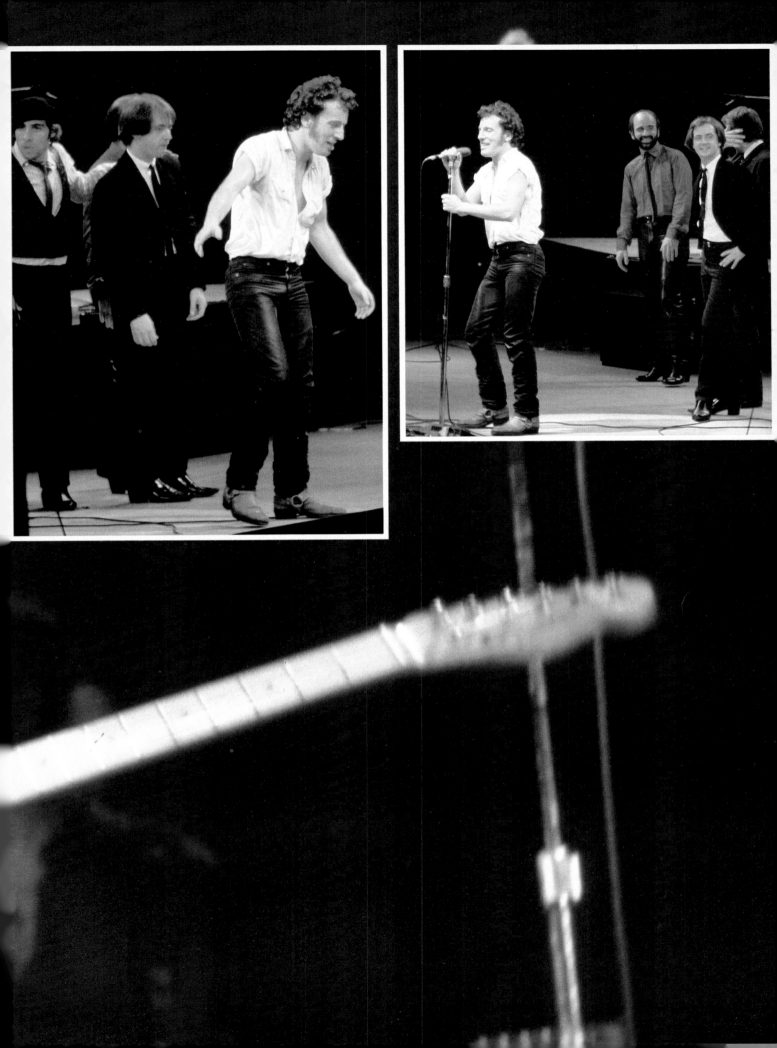